CW01551783

Tin Pan Arcadia

ROBERT SHEPPARD was born on the South Coast of England in 1955. Between 1989 and 2000 he worked on a long network of texts called *Twentieth Century Blues*, of which this volume is the largest showing. Previous books from the project include *Empty Diaries* (1998) and *The Lores* (2003). His work is anthologised in *Other* and the recent OUP *Anthology of British and Irish Poetry*, in which he is described as being 'at the forefront of (the) movement sometimes called linguistically innovative poetry'. He is currently Senior Lecturer in English and Creative Writing at Edge Hill College of Higher Education.

Previous publications:

Poetry
  Daylight Robbery, Stride, Exeter, 1990
  The Flashlight Sonata, Stride, Exeter, 1993
  Transit Depots/Empty Diaries (with John Seed [text] and
      Patricia Farrell [images]), Ship of Fools, London, 1993
  Empty Diaries, Stride, Exeter, 1998
  Neutral Drums (with Patricia Farrell), Writers Forum,
      London, 1999
  The End of the Twentieth Century, Ship of Fools, Liverpool,
      2002
  The Lores, Reality Street, London, 2003

Edited works
  Floating Capital: New Poets from London (with Adrian
      Clarke), Potes and Poets, Connecticut, 1991
  News for the Ear: A Homage to Roy Fisher (with Peter
      Robinson), Stride, Exeter, 2000

Essays
  *Far Language: Poetics and Linguistically Innovative Poetry
  1978–1997*, Stride Research Documents, Exeter, 1999

Tin Pan Arcadia

THOSE TWENTIETH CENTURY BLUES

ROBERT SHEPPARD

SALT

CAMBRIDGE

PUBLISHED BY SALT PUBLISHING
PO Box 937, Great Wilbraham, Cambridge PDO CB1 5JX United Kingdom
PO Box 202, Applecross, Western Australia 6153

All rights reserved

© Robert Sheppard, 2004

The right of Robert Sheppard to be identified as the
author of this work has been asserted by her in accordance
with Section 77 of the Copyright, Designs and Patents Act 1988.

This book is in copyright. Subject to statutory exception
and to provisions of relevant collective licensing agreements,
no reproduction of any part may take place without the written
permission of Salt Publishing.

First published 2004

Printed and bound in the United Kingdom by Lightning Source

Typeset in Swift 9.5 / 13

*This book is sold subject to the conditions that it shall not,
by way of trade or otherwise, be lent, re-sold, hired out,
or otherwise circulated without the publisher's prior consent
in any form of binding or cover other than that in which
it is published and without a similar condition including this
condition being imposed on the subsequent purchaser.*

ISBN 1 876857 89 7 paperback

SP

1 3 5 7 9 8 6 4 2

To Patricia

Contents

Acknowledgments

Poems from this collection were previously published in the following magazines: *Angel Exhaust, Anon Atextosaurus, Boxkite, Critical Quarterly, Cul-de-qui, Fire, Ixion, Lynx, Memes, Neon Highway, Oasis, Peggy's Blue Skylight, Responses, RWC, Shearsman, Sub Voicive Poetry, Talus, Tears in the Fence, Terrible Work, The Gig, The People's Poet.*

Others were included in the following edited collections: *A Purge of Dissidence* (edited by Robert Hampson); *Birthday Boy: A Present for Lee Harwood* (edited by Patricia Farrell and Robert Sheppard), Ship of Fools, 1999; *Horace Whom I Hated So* (edited by Harry Gilonis), Five Eyes of Wiwaxia, 1993; *My Kind of Angel: im William Burroughs* (edited by Rupert Loydell), Stride, 1998; *News for the Ear* (edited by Peter Robinson and Robert Sheppard), Stride, 2000; *Verbi Visi Voco* (edited by Bob Cobbing, Bill Griffiths and Jennifer Pike), Writers Forum, 1992; *Wasted Years* (edited by Robert Hampson).

Some were collected in the following pamphlets: *31st April or; the Age of Irony*, Ship of Fools, 2001; *Codes and Diodes* (with Bob Cobbing), Writers Forum, 1991; *Depleted Uranium*, Ship of Fools, 2001; *Fucking Time* (with Patricia Farrell), Ship of Fools, 1994; *Improvisation Upon a Remark of Gil Evans, for Miles Davies*, Ship of Fools, 1991; *Killing Boxes*, Ship of Fools, 1992; *net(k)not-work(s)*, Ship of Fools, 1993; *Soleà for Lorca*, Ship of Fools, 1998 and 1999; *The Book of British Soil* (with Patricia Farrell), Ship of Fools, 1995; *Turns* (with Scott Thurston), Ship of Fools/Radiator, 2003.

I would like to thank all the dedicated editors involved.

Melting Borders

Melting Borders

Preface to *Twentieth Century Blues*

Those buckets of blood there are the president's property;
they reek of recent history, but have nothing to do
with what has become your fault; leakages
of household gas that punch too-distant disaster-holes
in the indifferent sky. He'd skipped from jail to the
palace, rhyming with corpses that had fallen for him.
This is the first free bulletin for 40
years: his bullet-soaked face rolling
across the divisions of our suddenly parallel lives,
between striking ambulancemen and prisoners
handcuffed between 2 wall-charts: 'Given to Charity'
and 'Given to Shareholders'. Scab paramedics
give the *all clear* to the prostitutes' civic poses
in the glow from the ambulance windows,
after checking for small-scale social infections, now
8% of council tenants own shares. Why
these people come here, I don't know, great
gangs of lack of proof roaming across our lack of purpose.
One terminates every 2 seconds. Up
from the sewers, I will shoot into the celebrant crowd
until the fervent anthem of my machine gun
dies. I was a food-taster *and* sex-trap for him;
he took fingernails as hard currency. Violated orphans
like me are loyal to the people's secret brides:
old grain for sale in foreign-aid sacks, while you
worry about which gospel gives most truth,
where tangled colour-coded wires can be read
as misery-indices in 3-D; or where a pictogram of
a whale's tail dives into the charitable fund.

DECEMBER 28 1989

Smokestack Lightning
a mythology of the blues

for Tony Parsons

History of Sensation 5
Twentieth Century Blues 1

Let it all go. As I sing I drive my
dynamite for some strange machine
of this nearly spent century;
the big city calls its sinful
numbers heaven. My fast rolling
kisses are for the stern
lady, dodging me, back of the beat.
Our harp player's dead – when Pete
told me, we laughed. A quick shimmy
was Elzadie's goodnight; buttons and
belt loosening, Arvella's swift farewell.
Pete's 12 string steam whistle leaves town;
I want you to take my place in this song.
Elzadie lifted her hem and smiled, as he
tuned to an open chord. Bending G on the E,
the dog jumped into the horn as
the KC moaned, with a mocking beauty
mating rabbit foot dreams. Arvella slumped in
the shade, feeling contempt, thinking: give me
the train's shake. Sweat rolled off
transport as delight, a nervous fix
in this thief's paradise of form and
necessity possessed by devils. He'd
rehearsed all morning, restless,
couldn't wait to start again, to howl
out, temporal and grounded, 'We'll never
get out of these blues alive' -
above the frets, trembling. Inside:
shared diction, dancing voices, mojo stomping,
good book palms together in prayer. At night

she wedges the chair against the door,
feels evil thrashing outside the room,
but can't connect the pose of his
arpeggio muscles above her, de-tuning
slackening; sings down the phone:
'Take my lonesome love in hand.'
Dancing with her to the juke band,
his tense fingers practise chord shapes
up and down her spine; to be a real person:
a girl adjusting her skirt, singing *Twentieth
Century Blues*, a pearl on her lips, – her devil
astride two chairs, playing slide
with a Coca-Cola bottle. She
is about to say something over the
gossamer telegraph line, to survive
his strong hands rambling through.

Kid Bailey's the name I travel with, kidding
around: the name on the only phonograph;
walked up to the shop window, the glitter
of the diamond-fretted Dobro a death squad
tuning up. My handkerchief shields
the chord shapes from
your thieving eyes. Just pull the razor
and shave him. The gun in the guitar case was
no use – jealous man stepped up to Charley
as if to ask for *Pony*, retuned. Bill-
boards tell women what
to be: a circle of music-stands
dreaming thrills, dancing the Shimmy-She-Wobble -
some guy called it a dry fuck -
the guitar dances too, spins
above Charley's head. I could see
my own rapt reflection in the shine,
an invisible piano whose pedals are moody

bendings. Love my suitcase and the road.
Arvella's choked voice in his drowned
throat was only a name in a song. Late
capitalist machines filter hiss from old records.
White rooster corrugations beckoned Elzadie.
He looked at her empty shoes and built her up -
songs for gone Elzadie as he held
his guitar like an old woman he's just
drowned in the gutter. Arvella scowled
as I played his body, a piano's
grin, strategic melodic outburst. Suddenly
slashed Charley's throat, his light face
blackened to hell. Arvella leaned
against a tree waiting for the voice-thrower,
weeping as he watched. Dancing
flat against him, rising, I wanted him,
his cracked voice. Pretty girl, Bertha Lee,
a lot of Charley's singing for him, I thought.
Broken guitars above our heads, a scrapyard ceiling,
his breath on the damp trails he'd laid
on the backs of my legs. You could
make a plastercast of his hands,
real cobwebs playing host to a toy.
My skirts are grinning. His voice
is inside my sky, over the radio. Off
with nothing but my guitar and my name –
never played *Rowdy Blues* one time too many
the same barrelhouse. I spotted clichés every
inch of her body, chain-gang eugenics, a prison
which took your name. My thumb
print on his photograph; his words
want to lick me into the present – the tense
Son House always uses to speak of him.
Coming out of the Dark Road, the Silver Moon,
they look me up and down as though

I have subverted planking, beauty
that feeds off ugly draughts, a clinical
breakage in an imperial history. Pay
me faster, pay me cash, I carry you faster,
pay hot-love/hard-luck hobos who ride
the station wall. Dropping the needle was like
opening a door on his last jukehouse, nine-
teen sixty; old place I go, leaves trembling. . . .
When our harp player killed himself, he wrote
a three page suicide note, took a massive
no-mistakes overdose. Hold that woman I'm loving –
she's taught me to howl out the blue devils.

Suck the dominant zero of my shabby
industry! It's unacceptable trade,
sounds organised like oil-drums in a
car-wrecking yard. Guitar shell
across the knees, a glance
on the intricate drive toward death,
silence of too much music, condensed
like a dream in the assassins' streets.
My new harp wrapped in sore lips surges
in the body like the striped diesel bulleting
past that note before the fourth verse,
strings for the high wind to play silent,
gauging the tonic, fanning my hand
in the music's shell. We glowered
at each other, throwing shadows, our barrelhouse
quiffs turning from the keyboards. His hands
and my body spun web between the brothers.
Pete's guitar yearns a void,
cleanhead parody, suddenly chokes,
as she sings, accompanied by a trace of him,
driven to silence, floral phonographs on a coffin.
Arvella's face glowed, as the match flared. He

held it for a moment, glanced lazily, the ear
knowing the next chord pushed back to the dominant
and its rhyme, a limb floating the crowd.
Paralysed down one side now, Elzadie's
eyes had been splashed with tears,
the sounds of Cadillac death; Arvella's voice,
sweating the world it's breathed, his
teeth crowned gold. She's not seen Arvella –
the gasoline blowing black gusts above the
flames. She could still see the charred
frame of the cabin, blistering, red-hot, in the smoke,
and thought: that's over and the dream book's
closed, the strings nearly as dead as me.
Elzadie bit her lip, trembled, silent. What
stops the dissonance, the mad tears?
Dancers swim in my sound, here beyond
exchange, out of a deeply controlled accident.
The Schlitz sign was broken, flickered
as the dancers looked at her empty shoes
while I sang. Precision in the slither,
fixing mimetic fingers. He'd held the
guitar close to his body like a dancer,
trains re-coded as the soft roll
of her body, sparse wires following the track
more faithfully than a man will follow his love.

JANUARY–MARCH 1990/1993

Sharp Talk and Amended Signatures

Twentieth Century Blues 2

1

Thirteen 2

for Kevin Rowbottom

Sharp talk treats you like percentages.
Her red molar laughs, a kinetic suit
perched and purring beside her smudged lipstick.
Phatic 'For Sale' signs lubricate this
master and his mistress of the
post-colonial tea-chests. His ansafones
all breathe softly after the bleep, 'I'll
sort out a waterfall of hair' – but his
penis is working out tomorrow. It
barks for sex out of a gangster's
appetite as her body clinches jackpot,
their upended phrases jetting over the lush lawns.

Esher

Strategies 2
Boogie Stop Shuffle 2

Riot in terms of quantifiables on his communicative back stair-case. He's a shadow across the power-opulent heart of London as its alarm clock trills. A posing bullfighter minority of the tag-end

His speech is smashed out anxiety living in a postmodernist world of blowing kisses to everyone. You're next. Anyone with a black flag captivates her plural image

Minutes after looking at his penis, she steps up Church Lane, watches the map of symptoms. The deliberateness of the smashed panic. Four police vans of witnesses in perfect clothes

Commentaries in which the zeitgeist is ordinary perception, just things. A disruptive poetics is called for until morning's potential high tunings re-define themselves. A universal splashed against her window. The state snapped the sash cords

He realised that higher beings meant smashed officer gaps, a haiku fission, ripping through business. Young men with street recordings sat with fingers firmly over their ears. The screaming of a woman streets away

Trash car window tales of secret videos and tarmac wind to look over your élitist clothes. First class sucker knows the body tremor as she makes herself scripture. Libido sticks to her, chewing gum from a bus seat

The structure of gungrit and the side-street glimpse papers, moistened by rain. Rust-red brain tremors that run at the speed of instinct: frenzied emanations of BNP futures, off-peak utopias, entropic nets. Walkman refusals. AIDS terror choruses tuned into the skirt. The length of the slit is a corporate failure up festivals of commerce

Sex-show post-sleep apes void into solids. He wears my response on alert as he twists, in retinal delay, dangerous in his own body space. Hollywood big sleep with powdered style-perverts

Super-consumers hand-jive silence. His body signature votes in the language of limitless quantities for the blonde, who'd skipped off too quickly. It is difficult to speak to the hunter as the hound wolf-sniffs the cameras along the route

Busybody witnesses with perfect recall of events that will not happen. She weighs these rituals like a ghost. Her atoms don't appear. Resisting, she's framed in the L of the smashed-out window, massaging the struggle on all fronts

Slips on caked pigeon shit. Streets of mercurial wheels, of amended signatures. First out of the taxi is a can of Tennants, black high heels and the flashing knife, wrapping its weight in genital protection

Short-circuited, her fingers phallic, she wears the room in adversative change. He hoists the decoy of his erection, episodic or epic. They hold a dialogue of frozen armaments, communicative frames of men falling from ladders into competence

Keys were screwed into her. He licks her clothes slapped on her image, drawing the vulnerability of the day across her error. His clause assured her. Blood, still sticky, spattered their disregard

Stencils blot out the light as naked bulbs bleach the sun from the ceiling. His tongue bores a hole through her upstairs and it's banging on the floor. His head lashes, secure, from its appetites

TOOTING
MAY–AUGUST 1990

Codes and Diodes are both Odes

The Magnetic Letter 2
Codes and Diodes 7
Twentieth Century Blues 3

Invent icicles dripping interference
and discover structural lift
in emergent interchange
opening like a clam – multiply coherent
shoals of desire. Flashes classic Hollywood shot
in erotic slippage exhaustion,
scorched doors for release. Desire
dances in the polyphonic
sentence, means a world, slips through
the signified, refunctioned
in our critical hold: jigsaw
scales, particle syntax admitting
intertexts and music of rhizomic
diodes. Overlay of systems,
enough revealed delight to design
us all, while
magnetic words twin the
reader swiftly across echo's edge.

28 DECEMBER 1990

Killing Boxes

Melting Borders 2
Mesopotamia 2
Twentieth Century Blues 5

Soil keeps you in touch
on a piece of somebody
else's shit still turning on
that word beautiful isn't beautiful
torn in two directions transit
van debates wait for the
sunset just a blob to
me the arab shadows reality

Faces in the crowd emerge
from the emergency a confidential
whisper in my ear desires
peacenik erections on charts showing
positive coverage, as libidinal victors
curl tongues inside her want –
less convincing mumbling involves the
spinning rhetoric cares for you

Nothing erotic in this writing
except the writing kissing her
tattooed shoulder, lifting champagne to
long-laid hellacious phallicism, rubber
tents and missiles melting, penetrating
the mind favourable images from
art a war running with
the movie rights just run

Sand spray as a tank
dips a word gorgeous as
condoms over the gun barrels
the successful sergeant's string
of gassed canvas the network
sings open the window veto
there is a riot panic
printed on the contradictory winds

Behind that Union Jack curtain
the terminal fire-fly armadas
run pure liquid diagrams more
launch law than pilots dream
windows of the street rumours
of explosions at somnambulant destinations
focus the single man singing
the news through broken teeth

Listening to the combat fashion
the theatre smoke drifts across
boys on the piazza listening
to hours of hissing leader
tape passing the heads of natural
outrage. They have been
used, selling smaller dredgings from
costlier sparkles on foreign rivers

Hacked blossom in her withered
hand excrement lips at the
wound's edge butcher with a
body belt the eerie stillness
we talked about with sound
down it's entropy doubled anguish
waxing his arse fingers war
artist sticking to his guns

Take off to William Tell's
turkey shoot the script aims
and again the litany asserts
mundane miracles and monsters revving
into tomorrow wishful thinking in
inverted commas the roads are
impassable even here where the
apple spit hits my neck

Sealing realistic chances splashed by
chemicals far off you can
hear the sudden wet tracked
hiss of tyres running across
the mouth the bomb shelter
splinters like the words they
speak TVs without sound playing
to a room of men

Carrying bombs the way mourners
carry coffins he speaks as
a world president no slack
no slack fog grief teeth
biting through a smile hit
a cultural target the word
has disappeared a sacked fax-
man trauma kills euphemism flat

Victory rut discussed to technical
excess, it refuses to mean
this world, to eulogize the
glitter of local snow under
your divisional cage, implausible objects,
circumstantial happenings, slick shit clichés
win rhetoric, says the signs, read
your rich interdiction with collaterals

It's a lie. He rushed
off a blurred list of
names the mad laugh deep
from an insomnia that seemed
all surface sees during the
blackout of this news war
no voices lines crackling with
fleet laws for the sleeping

He's only one of many
postcards of cover shots the
rotorblades of smile in proper
poses of reason this night
is arrested and those bandages
will be collaged on those
vox pop cheering flash desk
men, recoding this masked desire

The sand's hot line burn:
wildcat smears under postmodern technologies,
t-shirts sporting these maps stretched
across camera thumbs-up, measuring
all manhood against princess warriors
in metal battle bras, jinking
oily luxury, dripping liberty under cover
of darkness or charred infernos

Our evidence for this? Wrecked
bent metal was shareholders' rig
dropping down tornado seed, war
pit monsters operatic talking heads
with smoke grained voices wild
weasel zap music as the
mother of instability crackles and
you hear the dream roasting

JANUARY–MARCH 1991

Slipping the Mind

Thirteen 3
Twentieth Century Blues 8

Slipping the mind
figments of post-
imperial assertion veering
off vanished skylines
invested window dressing
brown potted plants
the kick of
Capital each daybreak

Minister shoots from
slum avoidance nods
at arms deals
above a pool
ringed with rust
this moment not
repeated fireplace shorn
from a terrace

Coils of repeatable
citizens pouring the
eye 55 miles
of lapping propaganda
water colours over
this gutter pastoral's
precise assertion: *Liberals
Kill Our Kids*

1991

Weightless Witnesses

Empty Diary 1991
Killing Boxes 3
Twentieth Century Blues 9

To specific cultural targets under
      missile dances, they deliver genesis,
the meatiest burgers in history;

They launch scribbles from battlefields,
      thrust the agony shots: we're
prisoners 20 minutes each hour;

They print misguided sermons on
      Bedouin girls' torn shoulders, Justice
kissing pistons, lifting iffy weights;

They drop my stories in
      a quiver of blood, grunting
victory as the arrow falls.

1991

Soleà for Lorca

No song,
no, I do
not want to
see the duty
bound woman ignited
with touch as
men lead her
away, I want

to see the
wide camisole clouds

Silver icicles hold
back the night

I love you
gypsy (being watched

Car pulling up
outside, sharp silhouettes
under the lanterns

This time here
they come, branches
mute their sour
whistles

I love frost
shadows at dawn

tin lanterns shattering
day break

    Shouting
poet stumbling into
a pool of
star pocked walls

the flower of
these blood marshes

                         1991

Improvisation Upon a Remark of Gil Evans
for Miles Davis (1926–1991)

Put your flesh on
        a note, a bone
to be feathered for
        flight on the midnight
ride beneath my skin

     : ecstasy bites
in the fast lane

   put your flesh on

OCTOBER 20 1991

Fucking Time:
Six Songs for the Earl of Rochester

for Gavin Selerie

Phallic Shrines 2
Duocatalysis 11
Twentieth Century Blues 15

Dream of your eyes,
lips like leeches;
a wayward bullet invents
Fate as it

flies; worms twist his
armour; blood-scabs
on his prick. Appetite
leads, Aversion stands

off: peck and claw,
eye to eye.
She strokes fur; beauty
spots pock her.

Pissing fountains' vapour dances
before his milky
eyes, watery lids. A
million moments fuck

time, knotting the sequels
of pleasures, the
backdrop of fallen whores
and standing pricks.

'Phoebus tosses feeble shadows
Nymphs spoil for
frolics. The first deflowered
blossoms the ~~brightest~~

(*del.*)

~~briefest~~

(*del.*)

barest

Power and powder; blanched
stone in sunlight,
dog turds in shadowed
ditches. Leather dildo

spies the clap-sick
passions. Mares frisk
at the royal carriage.
She becomes coinage

of the realm, false
'incorporeal body', brisk,
pregnant, a bladder of
policy, bursting shit.

Saw the print of
her shape in
the grass, led the
coranto around Mercury's

frauds or Jupiter's adulteries,
leaf-mould hoof
rings where satyrs fuck:
shutters, mid-stage.

She spreads her fan:
her pearl fingers
frig lords. She performs
his dowry snatches.

Twist the pressure of
external things void,
a turd stirring beneath
her gown, perfumed

lice crawling a woven
scalp, mechanical fingers
scratching a lap dog,
two bitches licking

one prick; running over
an alphabet to
start a rhyme, warring
'tarse' against 'arse'.

Breath steaming, his thigh   ·
roasts at your
fire, lover's meat skewered
on butcher's eye.

Slap him like a
saddle, lewd engine!
Fat *bougre* in the
stocks, his neck

hangs like arse lard,
or fleshy backs
of old mistresses. A
beast, spitting sperm.

MAY–JUNE 1992

The Overseas Blues
: an allusion to Horace, Odes, II.i

for Harry Gilonis

Killing Boxes 4
Twentieth Century Blues 20

Startled eyes staring out of history's blank
wall its criminal phases causes, the fatal
      pacts of regional governors: pump-
      action shot gun points out
from the trees golden cartridges shitting smoke.

A dicey job bardic TV shows barbed
wire scratching sky, fire crawling on its
      belly across your minefield documentaries
      ashes over lava still aglow:
raw skin peels in your numb aestheticism.

Sheathed steel slips across solid thigh: jets
flash, horses frisk tails tied for battle
      flicking, limp hoofless home, alarm
      clock tabloids in media rubble;
leather crackles with light as they shoot.

Slave galley sails the coin's reverse: which
minefield is not manured with British blood
      ditches testify to war crimes
      blind lamps crash around Shi'ite
ears a single stain printing an epic?

Stop sexy Muse! leave history leave the
blues and the stink of these battles
        between your breasts I've killed
        for: Drip, in passionate expiation.
Sing, my plectrum feathering the dampened strings.

OCTOBER–NOVEMBER 1992

Shutters

for Jo Blowers 1
World's Body 2
Phallic Shrine 3
Twentieth Century Blues 21

Burnished fog of
daylight fleshes my
shoulder melts into
my gaze metal
bars to secure
the night
          fall
into the pit
OUTSIDE harsh discriminations
powder the air
with your disappearance
of light stolen
from the city
scabs of blood
bejewel each breath

They come out of the
darkness, men who watch while
they urinate, men who don't

          Cannot regulate their own brilliance
          digging out incitement from mirrors

Rituals we could not read;
our simple nobility an illiterate
wonder at the freshness of
their faces each stroke's pulling

at the small of the
back dresses a chair
the dream of a chair catches
the echo as a tunnel –

Ignore enough suffering for pleasure

Walking a riverbank: girls, our
other selves, bleached lovers' carvings
sparked, the glaciated distance veils

a sick trance
grassy carpets between
pleasure

and powerlessness fabric
not flesh
fabricated breath

tonguing veined cloth
Fold the shutters across

'He approached her from behind.
She felt a shiver as
he touched her shoulders. He
bent as though to kiss
her nape, bleaches her world,
swoons upon a draper's mermaid.'

I shivered. Ivy
mocked the sinews
of the dead
tree with its
crawling strangulations behind
which the workmen
were said to
relieve themselves I
clung picking the
bark off like
a scab this
drama of entry
and departure SHUTTERS
the light which
shores against escape;

is a cruel loan from
a sketchbook eye shivering privacies
                    tight. The thickest branches float
the red translucence of her
eyelids printed scavengers of avengers
plundered her pockets

elm's lightning

Her own mirror's violence, eyes out, finished,
sweeps across her illusion
                    streams across the
creases of perilous journeys
                    She is unfinished,
she is the ink of her confessions,
death's stiff drop
                    against the open shutters

in a stifled choke
       My fingertips press
throats, soaking your face in metallic light

a brittle dress
a battle dress
framing the door
from which he
captured his keyhole
THE STRICT DELIRIUM
combing the hair
long the body's
slow announcement that
it has life
that it has
to be perched
in this world
frames glare out
from the dead
EYES THE DEAD
landscapes our legs
did not exist
while the sweep
of the eyes
follows fabric's trench

'Men dirty and aproned, with measuring implements,
spades to trench the soft earth; wrists
flick ha'pennies on a board, slap weeping
women's faces. Window call it escape across
nothing, the eternal present of a winter

day's interior – shutters at last shut, bolt
across a schematic female beside the stars.'

        mirror's chill

        exclusion

            body steam

            floorboard shudder

I can look straight at you for
Once as a thief might
Between the public the public baths private
Lives were licked from streets
For exposure's slow sculpting; impossibility
ALMOST KNOCKS HER OFF BALANCE
My body a system of canals for
Fragile passion and passion's withdrawal
The pages uncut already crack open down the spine
Before the ridges of print you shall feel fabricated

    propped elbow
    collapses her back

    the deluge of
    green sunsets

upon the balcony's magnetised
drop

'A man wouldn't
know where to
begin to unhook
me a site
of moveable pathos

        Suddenly scaffolding half
        erected his London
        rushes in borrowing
        luminescence castaways on
        a window ledge
        we sew a

jungle of dust'

A halo flares
as the flesh
fails where screaming
light whispers to
the stars wild
eyed and domestic

The science of
solid fluorescence on
chemical starry walls

Between these escapes
I dream of
bodies scorched by
the STEAM of
the world where
decorum liquefies every
rustling Opera in
her chemise invitations
to sensual pits

A slant of
daylight penetrates, washed
the head against
dead STARS, black
as a flue.
I'm fallen like
a court dress,
a perfect conversation,
a lambent kiss

Mid-winter dusks blaze and then
freeze against the shutters her heavy
forgetting of legs an avalanche of
dirt in the weave of her
melting the memory of a voice
splinters the light in the flesh

1992

Flesh Mates on Dirty Errands

Empty Diary 1993
Fucking Time 3
Twentieth Century Blues 25

Her garters hook his
bullseye adorned for exposures
less human than her
latex condom mouth a
porn starlet with a
strap-on sexing her
second skin bruised with
verbs that frig their
nouns (*his anus flinches*
at my invasive breath

Gender collusion, uneasy meat

OCTOBER 1993

[37]

Magdalene in the Wilderness

im Angela Carter

Empty Diary 1994
To My Students 2
IM 4
Twentieth Century Blues 27

Weightless girl with bandaged wrists unthreads wolf
pelts from barbed wire posing for recessive
eyes which pose for themselves self-mutilating
innocents, nose studs bolted through freckled skin

Blusher dusts up her smile earrings shake
with next season's affront (a peeping tom
of his own shivers shakes his plumy
tail before her otherly army-surplus frame

Her robotic bleach-babes walk Capital's tightropes
sale victims dreading the hair perfectly transvestite
mix 'n' matching their grammars of perception
for the first fairy-tale after menarche

26 MARCH 1994

The Book of British Soil

A suburb an airport a park, named after him; a refusal to mean this world. Beautiful tracer fire, the bosses sweating. Shadows of unbroken factories, streets called *Alma* or *Trafalgar*

Two holes enface her disguise. He planted a kiss in the gulf between her shoulder blades. He initialled her corpse, a statue to the Iron Terrorist

The colony at the heart of the empire gets the news before the news: immobilised eyes stuck in skulls, ragged wounds to be filled; bathing in self-evidence, a sigh of immense national relief

Dad's big fist flooring Mum; she could be gouged from his fore-arms, burnt blue

There are no live casualties, soft-cruising over disused units

Look sexy for your sexy obituary. All the slips make the enemies friends, smudges of boot polish on the pillow

Each breath searches for its feeling. A rhythm of blows and kisses, she licks his thinking wound. He watches her sternly, selecting her skins from the shiny rails. Make up, making it up, with pencil and mirror, sweat erupting skin

Nerve agents work in a second. She kneels like a juddering protest whipped by rainbows. A nebula of blood cells behind her cloudy skin. His eyes, inland seas on a map of nowhere

A delicate hand waves farewell in the pane beneath the Union Jack. Recording tape hanging from the branches, the pop stars are re-building our sneers. Explanations airlift the empty hand of hand-shakes

Legible fear. *STAB HALF BREEDS* faded on the kerbstone

Tell this to the crying pilots: there are hulks of desertedness. At the stroke of nine, you reach the phone and the humming begins: Petrol is censored: Whitehall sealed off, eerie with snow

APRIL 1994

For Scott Thurston

Turns 4
Hundred 3.1
Twentieth Century Blues 32

where weathered

statues disdain the weather eye labours the
rustic scene scratched on opaque dawn scored
for disruption it shores up the weight
of the hushed world as condensed outlines

shakes their resemblances dubbed and dumb patterns
skin-damp with snared bird song annihilate
the moment's blossom on the *parterre* where
peace falls (we say) into paradise alone

unspoken a tongue on a downy lobe
steaming the sentient lock with its breath
and she turns to you implores you

be fleshed for her kiss only or
stands silent in shadow othered in stone
as a million suns scorch their mottos

NOVEMBER 1995–NOVEMBER 1996

Entries

for Jo Blowers 3
Empty Diary 1996
Hundred 3.2–4
Twentieth Century Blues 34

codes unrobed

tongue shooting pained bursts I'm as tall
as me on labels he sticks over
my fingers pussyfooting defiance ices my slaughter-
hole for his glans female scopophiliac rehydrated

gristle pictures in the body hidden from
my gaze as orgasm exits my face
shaves anxiety quivering his eyelashes with my
teeth *all eyes on his adjusted pouch*

frictionless richness with a perfect stranger a
flesh vessel that sinks us to shiver
as it's filled (anonymity cracks *yes please*

a pair of Fuck Me Shoes his
oily runnels unruly member he pulls back
the foreskin as though he is selling

womanliest denims

hug a quick release from his bite
nurturing his holocaust subjectivity I want him
my prickly understudy he's a milking touch
to mount a chair from his trousers

to leave no inbetweens all surface and
steaming sentient locks framed by black brastraps
double pleasures he never demands *my* gesture
lactates shadows shaped and held I enter

fingers lightly curled my long body pulled
negotiate *his* pushed out from the bedroom
nothing to enter slip doesn't shift I

kiss my glove with something mutual he
cannot see our bliss burns less brightly
than questions takes off: my dress: my back:

falls away:

without a hole he's left me elsewhere
everywhere nowhere I click his explosive pitch
his cresting a fallen phallocrat licks her
last portrait unzipped fat thighs prickling correctness

I close my eyes and I see
him dappled with gists (he says *Unpeel
her milky folds*) my display slips a migraine
clot in his brain replies *voyeuse*

doubleness gives him the look hell heated
the show's tryst I'm masked and I
will look myself wiped into a corner

how firm he sees himself shoulders tilt
the title shadows tremble his fist on
the accelerator of my throat muscles slips

MAY–JULY 1996

Ripping through Business

for Scott Thurston 2
Amended Signatures 2
Hundred 3.5 & 3.6
Turns 6
Twentieth Century Blues 35

I

he folds

a crease in smashing glass and broken
sleep. they think they choreograph shifting colonies
on the Common in gene pool superstition
a man in shorts watches the helicopter

in the night stinging beams where prohibitions
are fixed across the network of streets
he squats on its suspicion mounting the
air a ruined rubberneck twisting to talk

to the birds. tranquillities buckle as he
tosses a bottletop to a beggar who
hammers late into the night's yellow glare

pollutant humming the same structured uselessness fails
brittle smiles crackle over smart ID cards
turning on pain's map magnified in distance

II

grating the

nerves of the franchise constricting the chest
jingling in an atmosphere of shattered bottles
in a urinous alley for a wobbling
mobile's retreat the century's video of

naked statues mysterious tragic macho dumbo echoes
psychic key attuned to decay downs a
drop of Coke from a bin. lashings
in a hot pocket unlock the bomb-

factory in Woodbury Street (cannot find regenerate
routes through consumables diversions a missile a
light beam on eye-shields chopping over Tooting. . . .

as the moment's strain laps against you
consciously see this for the last search
among people not things *does not exist*

19 AUGUST 1996

Small Voice

Hundred 3.7
Twentieth Century Blues 36

darkness drags

a headlight's irradiated cone fading to an
English print of shredded lane rheumy vapours
tickling in time the throat catches on
slices of transitory purpose lost in decline

watch a row of identical open trucks
head somewhere archaic like a Midland colliery
not singing praises it's not even singing
the sharp rasp rustles in the ear

a redundant germ that drifts this Age
of Irony now happening to be forged
it barely sustains its volume of displacement
the vandals have fled   the gate bangs

scoop phlegmy lyric from the clogging drone
from the rusted hinges' lament

bitter croak

JANUARY 1997

Small Voice 2

for Tim Woods
for Scott Thurston 3
Hundred 3.10
Turns 8
Twentieth Century Blues 39

lightness blooms

do not interrogate the taillamps's eradicated drone
voice within vision musicates, released ears entune
its captive turn, the others no longer
fixed in the totality of permanent waste

this pleasure animates a knot of rapturous
ruptures mass graces *follow me* dirt from
itself: erotic or aesthetic it prises each
permission without distinction tinkles in shivered delight

*We don't live in Utopia but glimpsed
it for one moment*: the daily catastrophe
anchors an epic ethos in liminal illumination,

audial; orchestration of things covered by
a grating the 'utensils' remain compound;
windows spring black roses in en-

visaged articulation

JUNE–JULY 1997

Variation and Themes
dedicated to the memory of William Burroughs

IM 6

Twentieth Century Blues 40

Alphabets, 15 feet tall, spell their shadows across the Pavilion lawns, before the Gate of Heavenly Peace. The shell of some other purpose opens and closes like a comedian's false teeth, the optimum moment for a billowing event whose meaning is drowned. Dying, sprinkled by the arms of a floral clock, mechanical flowers sprout from a bed of zinc and acid. Genetically engineered on the Downs near Lewes, it was selfish to have created these analogues, to have found pleasure, doubled, thereby diminished. The paratexts, the end of season rust, of staples, could buy up his epic marginalia, stretching the adjectives, never allowing the text closure. He surely deserves to keep something open, a verdict, to get her to try its impulse, just to see which triggers are released. Undetectable wood from trees, sheep from sirens, flesh-coloured drizzle. Listen, Rubbermouth, your insides turned independent. Sewage nettles can cure the sting – without doubt. It was her idea, sensing a morphology of slogans to take on the quest in which, she realised, she was no Aphorism. The formal function blazes his path. Gathering a sense of injustice the authority of intention flickers an alibi, or witness, tempered by the stenographer's fingers. Back in its shell, the jewel sheds its history. Eyes screwed for her signal, as do people around. I fanned out my passions, as though an allegory of timelessness. Listening to the second, she was free of me, for the stage composed the season. Grunting at her head resting on a copy of Blake's poems, the wrong proper noun was another affair altogether. Somewhere I hear the murmur of *book thirteen*, which skids the interpretations, the history of the last soaked stage. Particulars matter, fall invisible to earth, and blow in the sand: alter ego dust. The Other, invisible, was startled by the light pouring contaminated responsibility or its lack through the suddenly open door, erotic or thanatognomonic. Whatever it is, into its blaze stepped an

[49]

outline of something feminine, whose contours were bled by her breasts, an immaculate conception. Its prefatory flagellations seem like so much verdant perversity, though off-stage. Map undulations, as you lay there, dialogic. He could still order her to stream into the rivulets of her clothes' breathing emerald, in a last appeal. She stood, deep in shock, weeping into a clenched fist, her knuckles marble. Observe the approaching rituals of locality, served up urgent. The gas they bottle is obdurately untraceable after the hood has been donned. THINK misadventure. Anagrams of several girls' names entertain themselves. And then the ultimate enigma, in a dignified preparation for frenzy: the mourning sky, black clouds scooped and fluffed by skilful hands, physics rushing towards art as if it were the last helicopter out of Saigon. The last governor cast scented shadows. You treated your dot in the sky, constellated with a pattern they called History. Bulbs of Memory bob in its fluid, definitive guesses, youthful renditions of surprise. Brimming actuality is the demolition crew's meat. A twisted, unrecognisable mammal chases its tail, gobbles its own shit. After ten thousand spins, you're listening to pure dirt, something triggering undifferentiated stench scissored from the word *latrines*. The popular front for the liberation of antique consciousness. The broken clock, showing this, proved little more than a right time for the utopian parliament of pure sound. The Pleasure Brigade was drilling. His wall a perfect blank, he wishes somebody else could reorder the fragments upon it: windows of the spray-canned New York memory is lyric. Rest between the paradigms, the consciousness of glue, vulval palms displaying drying limbs sticking to surfaces. Diego Rivera of a world turned inside out, a mausoleum of melting snow. Nobody feels the need, scrapes adhesions from this instant he's left without. Emotive dust reconstructs the body; he's chiselling a shout from the street for its outline. Something like sex, in the earliest years of getting his body to move, unable to contain it; something like Fuck Musics, rolling the captions of what is, a transparent dumbshow building characters, becoming the crowd's gaze, a miraculous medium all signifier. It jumps once, a conundrum almost solved. Tombstone: trombone, the long notes of the wrong truth running analogues of this justified but unjust, inalienably real, scope. A bargain intruder bursts through your door, demands whatever there is left with such free information passing for particulate matter, toxic enough to dispose of a promised hero, gifted beyond volition. Struggling inward, sucked from the pen's bruising. The brain's rind is caked with glutted machine dust. Cod piece, minus cod. A windsock filling with torrential passion scared him off through the fabric, exhibiting himself to himself. A simple mind inhered, each fresh sheet of carbon has survived. Footprint in the cement, an island for the rain to fill. Non-entities without terms, wordy expositions of the realm. Headlines fucking or comparing themselves to dreams. Her grandfather was a Bolshevik. She bent over the easy chair as he walked in devalued currency, a Baptist entering water. The melting exchange of her dowry: the bark of a dog strangled on its chain, a blossom at the second decimal point of the penultimate equation. Each thought is literally addressed to proving himself himself. Take the number of your feet! His perceptions no longer blent. In his least favourite account of the world it was total. Once in a while, a disappointing hero declares personhood. Bus back a face-to-face, the birth of saying must never close its naked gluttony for what is said. Thought's eunuch watches her masturbating. It touches this paper, spills in helium shrillness, insinuating threats to your integrity. Where else does a date live, but in cannabic shadows harbouring your least favourite implicate ordering, the Paranoid Passiontroopers? Consciousness, out there, isn't, wasn't, *law* with a Capital L plate. The false equation trails you home, leads space probes into black files. You stand at Stage Two and wait for the lights to go up. The end of the calculation is a Prologue. The rest is History. Accelerations by greasy fingers. Celerity a constant assemblage. No style. Minus poetry. A deadpan calligraphy, the larvae shot into the thyme bush where they were mistaken by red ants for their grubs. Deep in the critical inquest, Otherness burst at frantic captors. Police helmets score through media, webbed with pollen. His palms adhere to brick, pre-emptive Metamorphosis under mirror attack: too large: smells bad: obviously alive. In other words, a story. She cements a gargoyle into a hole in the punch floor of focus, though nobody watches at first. He draws the attention, gathering papers, stony-faced hologram, post-partum monstrosity picking his nose. He's gone, invisible, in the anthracite, the decomposition chamber. The other side of glass speculates. Webbed in with coincidence, it leaks, dampens a rôle glossed in a footnote. She can have Centre Stage! She can complete her ferocious revenge that shocks still. Under gnarled fingers in the silence, the keys stop. History waits and can just make out the car. Your memory is less and less slipped over. Thumbprints on the bonnet have just uttered. The other half of the life spent the person as somebody else, frowned on by this glowering self-evidence, an inefficient grip on this rush to summary and physical integrity. Vomit a shadow on the wall. Her spontaneous evaporation washes a recognisable terrain, the inky rim in the bath. In and out of static they almost receive an instruction to catch the drowning voice. It befalls you, as nothing more pertinent than a re-naming, black noise edging every statement you'll make, the inhuman whistling of solar flares. Wallow for attention in the gulf of the voice's extinction. Disconnection of all visible circuits, like guilt, like conscience. The addition of less and less until the ancient stenographer rattles pure pitch. A hard punishment disfigures the waves, not a shiver, safe from its play in a pun on the word *Justice*, the undeconstructable, unerasable, final card, when the chips are down. You are not in this story with its yapping clues, its ethical pivot. It wants to gobble your pocketfuls of rhyme.

JULY–AUGUST 1997

Dialogues

The Collected Works of Josef Stalin

brush my cheek my whittling throat

the fisted rosebud (iron
plough and the voice of the poet

open. Obey.
Land sing praises

voice: filial lily
        kicked in the guts
breaks its
neck snapping breeze

duty breathing song

the chained earth: :moon hushed smiles

great daylight (begging

his shadow

teasing the horizon

tatter the forest startled
life
spills your *head cannot hang* the hermit

returns haunts a tomb-blank

detained by hope

ghosts

knock us up

poison

the lute clinks (selfless

song in its own praise double
scented

no joy dropped
in its darkness No

false shaft of grafted song

entwined heart's

harp. snarled.

no passion drowns

in its luck

   (crowds
resemble, chant
blank exclamation marks

25–26 September 1997

Ten

Flick of hair on a glistening.

Ashes collapse dust blanket Ah!

Seeing apertures adjust.

Glances through the chickenwire.

Devise admissions to self.

Torn into transcendence? Rending

Despair see

Ekeing out

(tensile)

. grinding against bone. grand

. .

Out in the kitchen.

'An ethic of pleasure in the shadow of responsibility

Looming edifice. Spring rain

Drenches you in promise learned as premise

Kiss my skills

!

Says ashen snags on wire the scene keeps changing the curtains.

Pocked surface, rain

pitied. teasing-

hovers over a raft of projections

.

Ripping through vision, torn sheets; flapping image-shreds slap
       the day in the face.

Leisures' measures'

Blossom blissfuls of.

(Sighs!)

Hand falters over the contract.

Sign a size too few.

Sing a shock a

Abolish . . .

I'm all eros, prosthetic rust!

9 OCTOBER 1997/2000

Beginning with a line from a Chinese poem in an English dream

Twentieth Century Blues 44

at last the lineated look that was me playing in a palace or a cage
neither a musical instrument nor an ancient board game so
beautiful we forgot the locked door though caricatures rushed
through the bamboo gates

explode onto petrifying talk of freedom a mouth that hollows
out allegory like apple blossom like the lamentable loss that
was who

at least the line took me away to wrestlers in flame less to the
threshold which bled my smarting eyes into a bowl extenuat-
ing my ear as identity's howl

just a fluffer to stiffen up the hero for the heroine who arrives
so long the appetizer burns off across the polished codes or the
skein across the keyhole mucoid glue that stuck in our eyes

sticks in the grain of the throat the frozen limbs of the rivers
after extensive searches through identical slats of bridges below
where naked men bathe in the ladies' identikit confessions

pointing with his folded fan to the warm up act lest your limi-
nal luck should run out to the rearing horses and be trampled
to a thirst

to the leasehold of *me again*, O line invisible, I weave my mutest
lip from the gloss

16 OCTOBER 1997

Sonoluminescence For All

cell deaths in our faintest bin users mismatching

no testicles pseudodecorate

regulates the cross reaction signalling (array)

bite faced drops evolutionarily open

germline Sefton coast phages

nearly face on binary turbulence corrects your frizzled family down

but I don't believe in wasting the mantle is shaking error

Cadaver! I'm not condoning execution

message detection kit off to the shatter of a redundant truth

rodents and Man. Subsoil

pinhole fantasies with wild bioethics

no noise free images resonate downstream

information cascade scaled individuals

your favoured site of Heineken bottles replicate one's body's own
photo cleavage misconduct

hypermutation game in the Name scooting ropes of signature

a just rapid changing temporal informing manipulated left hand lie

26 OCTOBER 1997

Armchair Adoption

Dialogue 4
Twentieth Century Blues 46

: for surrogate twinness the Palatine does

sell it! On the really mat, bands
of nattergirls. Cast casteness
on a bonelit transparency
flipping the mono-ness channels. Wipe
no-ness and less than no. It's

a boy: she's a girl proves

it; gagging gift of existence, literacy
is not just for life. *Fatty's got a real thing
and not a dead thing.* Cough up a certain one
lineness. Download
the Person as Absolute Theme

You do it. *nessness*

OCTOBER 1997

In Good Voice

Small Voice 3
Dialogue 5
Twentieth Century Blues 47

A poem always accepts the conditions of virtual dialogue
JACQUES ROUBAUD

rainbows
frozen across the floor

crumbs for me – *n*,
for example, spectrum strip

from the voice's delights. ***Take one*** outside

'I'll fix my inverse position for
whoever. Houselights screen a possible calm

master the me
speaks only up one moment

inner *which*
yet the next unhinged you

where negotiations in practice

you *when* in theory
willed by shape perfect caked in time

'Not sure whether this act is squeezed,
something to slop out behind an invoice

in the duo's
trash intonations

tooled you (or me) rust
of the un-re-en-visaged

assertion
questions history's other croak

the shadow's turn off as real as

nature takes the refracted seat
in this answer back

any vehicular position

shit-heap casualties utter relations

'Accounting flutters from
ethics sure as Hell. *Follow*.

into unofficial darkness

too close to the icon eye it
filled in somebody else's archive

so long So and So!) 'Don't worry, we'll
uncover our tracks before

setting out the double columns

you give a little pleasure about aboutness
dead reader haunted (*voiced*

30 OCTOBER–6 NOVEMBER 1997

Dialogue between Created Pleasure and the Resolvèd Soul

for Ben Watson
Dialogue 6
Twentieth Century Blues 48

Not you again, you big
girl's blouse! (cleaving twist and twain

Concretely uttered, may my light executive
dusting be considered as a form of life?

There's none in that body, all hooks
and spin, as PC as a veiny dildo
humiliating the inner voice, king of things

Dead systems twinned, halos
monumentalise the air

Speech, pure dictionary in double split
sides, inseminates the shifting
axioms of material in an outcry.
If you want
an interesting interior life get up
off your fat arse and get a
job you aphasic blank. Blink.

Fluid category fleshpots utopia.

Don't speak (to me) with a corpse between
your teeth, bumping into (and off)
yourself in fatal leather snapping
in twos and toes as I seduced you with picket
grace whims cross-dressing as a 39
inch bust in centimetres. Mutter
mutter mutter mutter (falls into the social

come
dark
shot
grapple
hardcore
vice
versa
joint
stock
sublime
fudge
dog
organs
being chained to the fucking cosmos
tackle
the quest
to beget
better
sex guides lay back and think of the stars

Sample that bitch, a small
simulacrum of somebody else's else. No
code?

No ode – just the behaviourist's crystal.

Polyphonic ejaculation! Do you
want to handle my swollen gland; in
my language we have the same word
for 'man' and 'girl', for 'love

'dream

'knots

'not equal

'objection

'size

'='. You *can* teach pork
to snout the spot

Pleasure as an idea is a
formula. Anarchy as a theme
is a juice derived from shot.
Spirit a bucket.
            Diametricalism
as force to be reckoned is a
gang rove in tense invidious.
Matter is muttered all about
'you', you hoodlum of the lip.

I don't. She
discerned the hand of a man

decisive, dark, menacing,

on the envelope. I'm trying to
fill a thriller at the moment
with knowledge as human as death

Your tropes bellyache tripe
as trite bathing belles sharked by conscience,
etymology as any sighting?
Discourse on trees,

weed dust explored mistaken

uli.

ex

–land

(wrack):

puritan shrug-offness meets bursts of
busting
statutes and ripe rips
cul-de-breach
and a whole bunch of jingle-lessnessness
(again)

category-collusive coughs between movements

Please God, don't erect me when
the doctor grabs my balls, situated,
endowed with meaning and hating it.

Let's get right inside the outside,
the neuro-ideological poem
that spits out its writer,
well no or yes
about four hundred times a year, its
responses corrected through liturgical
marginalisation.

You said it. No dialogue
without thinking with the solids.

No job too small, the will not
down the pan. Lift
the lid on the eye: chaos patterns
in the bloodshot rolling,
an ecstasy that shatters the bloom, showers
petals above the literal ground;
on a wet, black chop.

Bliss my chora! Tort my chorus,
Trot, whiz-sin pinkies fan the air

(O harmonicas in your little
plastic coffins, arise!)

Be inside everywhere; outside
the booby boom

that spot that get us hot, you and I.

The 'metamorphosis of the materials', you mean?

13 NOVEMBER 1997

Tin Pan Arcadia

borne witness by the hissing
faster than gone
distributing oppressive music as
twitch for rebellion
a note on the step
for the proletariat
on the mantle of shine
explodes the stylish syntax of
devouring privatised eye
the anti-mirror shatters
freedom tastes of limits
speaking oracles
from a signed edition
a hush too far to mention
fascinates *their* tarnished utopia
an apocryphal critique pricked
into skin or a sculpture of
Pol Pot crafted from skulls

20 NOVEMBER 1997

Towards a Neo-Diagonalist Manifesto

power is wrong (you better enjoy it
next week's metanarrative is *phuttilized*
to a crispy post-trauma! (spindoctors
gridlock our sweaty horns as we cough
up the nightmare they swallowed
we don't conceptualise
the big princess in quite the dress
on a very small blackboard
inside off onto numbered
opinions dumbed down for the night

27 NOVEMBER 1997

In the Room of a Thousand Mute Salutes

Mute Salutes 1
Dialogue 9
Twentieth Century Blues 51

Jewel up to trembling
hypotheses hybrids crown their brazen verses

sublime re-affirmations of all that can be said

just by watching men grunt the Earth. For example,
East facing behaviours and blank relics in the bedroom

mutate into a tradition you barely unmute

Earth is a colony of its own future. Sex
in verse: boy-slits strangle your testes, veiny friend

The soldiers fall on their booted-up whores
wrestle with an elaborate rhyme scheme

Earthen birds twitter
the anthem of some migratory Muse

(And her shadow

DECEMBER 1997–JANUARY 1998

Re:Entries

Entries 3
for Patricia Farrell 3
Dialogue 10
Twentieth Century Blues 52

If milking a stretch then somewhere someone's demanding
a slide, catching a glimpse as catches

Nothing that's been reported but bladders huddled in bed, singing
to each other along the route to soak a crinkled vein

Stemmed for dressing, enact upon a
leather fringe. Derive:

A tongue drags its appreciative lap-routes all
dialogue resistant

The night had a thousand oils but it doesn't
repay the compliment by varying its
vocabulary of return caresses

Ideality peeps undignified shots wish a length *the* length of the
room shooting pencil-thin through the keyhole
out to useless gobs for shiny hides
or beyond!

Bitten pout bitch moistening synecdoche in figures, pads
for spilling cushions under a million
dreaming glans) *gone snap*

Unfold any passion could have spilled across one leg, the
narcissistic
floating, the laughter of a spy!

If the tongue's trail entered an entry without a thought,
leaves no blood on a milky thigh, then there's
no story without telling, another
day of congealed gloom

If orgasm digs pianoforte tongues across the weight of
frown, then near-entries float mounds
around a landscape in top

The body doesn't release words: they arise in the eye like love's
temperament, muscled
black, titles of hunger pumping on tip-toes, sucking hard on the
hard!

Calming the traffic of delivery jolts on the
bumpy road towards never
covering the traces

11 DECEMBER 1997

Freeze It

I would have preferred to sing the blues in any small bar full of smoke
than to spend the nights of my life scratching into language . . .
ALEJANDRA PIZARNIK

I

Sonic topology of certain unbearable blues threatens to turn out
onto Kingston. Suits shine with human contact notes set up
with yet another rehearsal rolling. I look unlikely in this accel-
erated context: Chris and Tony unload vinyl. Thrash ear-pressed
harmonica plays the rainy drive, caverns filling with noise and
satellite TV cutting the night into uneven strips. A monstrous
chord fills the room bounces back and forth across the lips
programmed under flat-out Capitalism the leisure to read
poems. Pulling it played the last line for Duster Bennett.

II

Flesh and blood miked catching itself. More with the body
coming up to peak, sweet. Help me as memory in sweaty dreams
lacks signings to pink shows, coming home tired (to Tooting).
Elzadie's noise off again lost in finger skills catching herself in
time as in sex concentration upon images themselves without
howling *where is she?* Brash chorded little-voiced harmonica ears
hardly hear her felt so bad with his intention-equivalents that
she devastates and overtakes. 'Then vote something else! Or
nothing.'

III

Playing is literacy prettily missed. Silent vibraslap in Chris'
gloved hands, my gaze slo-mo, turning harmony-manager.
Convention joke's not played a mysterious youth power recap-
tured. Middle musics rescued our time in the room to 'do' the
total songness. Antiquity's waste burns timely in a *de-vinyl*
belted raincoat economy! I miss the riff Peter Hope-Evans puts to
bed for me. It's one instrument, it's two: yet others say six!
Homunculus! Three-quarters mattress will do it: cliché errors
in however wherever no-time styles.

IV

No time for listening I haven't sung. I cannot write from
Hambone's vehicle, fingers on the fretboard, soft, lost in image.
(I take 2.) I've been helped minutes before writing this stolen by
1936. We play in versions as two keys act a voice (simply) through
me. Reverent reverberations laugh compensate with the stock-
ing tops of Mussolini's granddaughter. Roses on harps confirm
my perceptions with time phantoms not dissipative with
Charley Patton tuned sky high! Haunted with grace I hear the
liquefaction of the hangover trying on an ethnomusicological
wheeze: piles of out of tune harps on Sonny Boy's grave.

V

This remote narrowcast we called Arvella in monochrome as he pulled it from Elzadie with excitations of the wide-eyed sweet thing. Documentarists play years awaiting lucrative tears as smut never proved their probity to Willie Mae. Gutted carpets fit the manager like Labour Party posters sealing self-absorbed imperial shines. We've had enough. She weeps regally as *Britannia* sails from the only colony she has left: the British People.

VI

Listening to Tony sing, refunctioned into *Briggflatts* (reading after the gig), tingles each time I mime, sheer jam swung guitars swept the floor between the Out of Date and History: hereabouts Every Day; you'll find me talking to myself, downtown, like somebody else. I'm forcing myself to not imitate burnt-out words in my heart, as Peter Green realised every time.

VII

If the wind should change, then fiduciary belongings amount to two dozen diaries. This romance surrounds you, this late century blues in an unplayable pack of quotations in quotes; crude effects play oddments' tricks. They've got another bill, poisons of crimes, looking from musician to musician, transposing keys: a guerrilla tactic somebody's aching fingers will track and hammer to death, night after day after night.

VIII

Blown lament returned laughing nor did Jo Ann Kelly's dead
arm blues. Courage spools travelling blues squeezing eroticism
rambling through your smooth voice at its last letter's elemen-
tary harmonica stance. *Sung* in *Snug*. Used its riff, listening walls
shake with style-rut not barrelhouse; inexpressive as the wine-
dark riverside.

17 DECEMBER 1997

The Push Up Combat Bikini

A Hundred and Eight Robinson Crusoes

FRIDAY: MY SECRET LIFE

Kick into heaven or hell my heels squash Crusoe's chips

But he'll be a good doggie and gobble my flaps

With the curve of his penis and the swelling of his testes through his rubber body suit

he'll package the dog's bollocks unto dust

His muffled voice from the pillow

He rogered *Matron*?

Thursday and I scratched SOS on his inflamed back and mounted him howling

'Surely, not even Thursday could stiffen at the adhesion of this songbird's beak

What if a dancer, her sharp breath spangling the frozen air, should spring from one almost weightless sleigh to another, pivoting on a handstand, to leave a single print?

When the helicopter crews realised we were new kinds of human being they roared off in disgust

I squeezed Crusoe's limb until it was black and ready to drop or
feathers would squawk from its tingle

Used that Howler Monkey Trick I licked yoke from a turtle's egg
pressed between his buttocks

Blowjob round by the garages

gripped her peroxide tuft with one hand and counted pieces of
eight in his pocket

(*Thoughts microphone:*) You are my Hero, I have made you, out of
nothing etc

Exquisite artifice of terror: a hand adjusts the wad that pads your
mouth

I gripped the chair-back and felt his milky gaze flow across my
rump and back

in time to his curling snake breath

''Blow me up and fuck me,' that's what your label says!'

(he said

SATURDAY: CHEMISCH-TECHNOLOGISCHER ROBINSON

He boils cockerels into tarpaulin

Knits bags for his Hoover spins feathers into handkerchiefs

The sink-plugs in Crusoe's bathroom are breast shapes pierced through the nipples with rings, chained

'Oh! Your heart is a spear your stars are targets

(If *this* is 'what *she* wants' then it is wanting

As director I shall shoot myself cut myself back in

His balls in freezing sacks he pissed in the sink

A dead phone chord round his neck, face covered in tin foil and polythene

monadic self-sufficiency

he'd slavishly choked on Thursday's perspiration

The sucking sound was probably only blood passing greedily through his appetite

(Sings, operatic:) *The evidence of my debauchery/Will be lying in your mortuary*

SUNDAY: CRUSOE IN SHORT WORDS

'Doc' Crusoe's blue lit scenario aroused my nosophiliac eye

After I'd changed him, I jerked him off with a parrot glove
puppet

'Mistah Kreutznaer – He Dead

Little world from scratch sloppy as ever as to principle

Your black thoughts mounted the First Musket

Restraint was breath control of a subtle kind

(*Whispers:*) Angela McWhirter's
            glandular squirters

impossible to meet you

                    Thursday

But why this prolonged hunger?

Oculinctual mumbles of this blind fidelity at my mascara's edge
scour the chalice of my fake chastity

My bikini-bottom is up before he bursts in on the dot of the
Shipping Forecast for his goat-roast

steaming

MONDAY: CRUSOE INFERS

The Vessel Captained by a Man of Quality yet Manned by a Young Pup:

Lipstick for his lips

Fishpaste for his teeth

Gnaw at your drift with human eyes

Monday to Friday

Musket Number Two was for the fermenting impression you found next to your wine-press one morning

'Is this the Hand of God?' you asked, falling to your knees

It is the print of a woman's etc

(Ideas in English relate to other ideas solely

'Four legs produced this big dog with a mane of human hair

Shape of bone is an innate notion that hangs between (or even *within*) species

as a threat (Good

as a promise (Evil

as a bendy plastic doll without a prick (Undecided

as a vinegary old tart melting into her component chemicals (_____

TUESDAY: CRUSOE THROUGH THE LOOKING GLASS

Hunched over his polaroids

Click!

'How *do* fishes masturbate?' mused the actor in *Siesta for the Fiesta*

My latex eyes infer his potentiginious kink

(I read it for him

(It moved this afternoon while you were out alone thinking

From experience they are effects of custom hissing the sunburnt human flesh on heat in his hands

A bottle of plonk on the beach and Robinson 'Pretty Boy' Crusoe (in nappies) sucks melting jelly babies from between my toes

(Sings:) *I wannabe an amputee/ and lose my leg below the knee;/pulled from the wreckage of my plane:/I will never walk again*

Robinson 'Long John' Crusoe hops around the yard dusting his knee with the season's precious flour

The Thursday bird cooed: 'Ecouterism

Paperweight which held down your Problem in probability I remember well winched open on your desk

So she could suckle me with blood used Crusoe's last razor blade to gouge me another mouth a Truth Hole

(*Reads:*) 'Year 17: Breasts like bells they carry the pot of Irish Sea
stock to the leopard carcass

The shape of those ideas

Crusoe's mind-forged callipers measure each for Science

WEDNESDAY:

Le Dernier C'rousseau

Grumpy bride perched on a tombstone for congress

Whipped his swelling goats each time they nibbled my PVC miniskirt

I thought: Give The Dog A Bone works both ways

'Shrink his breeches and damn his eyes

Crusoe the Cat thought: 'Deceiver: dog as a god

'Hush Bedwetter

(my glove heavy on his zipped mouth

'Musket Three . . . that was for the single handprint you found midweek in the frost, at midnight, stumbling midway between the pub and home

There was none

A card for the Meatotomic Club is tucked behind the dialling information of the island's single payphone

'Lick this live flex

THURSDAY: THE ANTIC ROBINSON

I love that remote control around my fingers yet there is nothing to control now you are gone

Elegant Subterfuge

(*Thinks:*) 'Any woman who has had it with a dog would never again be satisfied with a man

Why these untenable metaphysics, a mutilation scar tucked in for the night

Crusoe the Kid's cool exit west

The blank screen dreams my update of your docu-soap

The full squirting vision or the strange kind of rescue

The Triple Blast of Muskets, as Thursday accidentally trips over the Security Rope

Synchronises a legion of panoptical devils

(as planned

Canned Laughter

I dropped my new top unzipped his slits so he could see the undulant slogan:

'*Castrate Lactophiles*

                              (we learned to read
              in the women's toilets

(*Writes:*) 'Year 23: Gave birth to a playmate, a bitch as sullen as myself: Tuesday

Robinson had flipped to that old TV Crusoe again, badly made in black and white

She taught Thursday to talk like the parrot despite his enduring Priapism his pungent sweat

(beyond the Pale

One of the Crusoes had warned, 'Don't breathe my sperm over Thursday

(as somebody unscheduled, like me, slipped from between his sheets

January–February 1998

Downing the Ante

Articulates 3
Killing Boxes 6
Twentieth Century Blues 55

A cold genocide counter-solved the heel

Seal the borders the studio audience *can* and *will* weep when women feed for oil

Says Mr Casablanca

Scorched stiff in his white socks

Not fussy where the operatic commas go on the wire copy

Flat out fax attack beneath the spinning radar

(The facts drowning in formation

30 MARCH 1998

Abjective Stutter Expectorates Laugh of the Human

for Jo Sadler

Utopian Tale III
Internal Exile III
Human Dust 3
Sharp Talk 3
Magdalene in the Wilderness 3
Lores and Bye-Lores 3
Articulates 4
Empty Diary 1998
Twentieth Century Blues 56

. . . . boards the bus in a rush, hot; removes coat, jumper, puts

Coat back on, adjusts shades. Her cropped, gelled, hair, dyed black,

Free, suggests youthful self-possession, reveals *how* she is suggested

In a narrative believed to conceal 'consumption's salivated excess'

:'My hot meat on a half-bus seat

:'My floppy jockstrap leaks ego-transgression

:'My hysterical kidneys sweat blood as hyper-masculine glory gifts!'
'You're

Loaded with waste, larded with fear!' she laughs, tips this favoured tripping

From those ventriloquial lips. The bus stops, half-empties

Opaque bodies hoist themselves aboard; fills. She gives

Her seat up to a disabled human, moves back, mirrored, towards

Others: the glitter of a self, doubled. Care of self, of rings and
ear-rings, nose-

Studs, minimal eyeshade; shells. (Let's announce: <u>It's taken
nearly one hundred</u>

<u>Years for her to fall in self-less love with herself</u> (*Ha-ha, has it?*

7 MAY 1998

Angel at the Junk Box

im Frank Sinatra

Midnight Ride 3
IM 7
Twentieth Century Blues 57

I

Breath betweens the sexy brass
quakes against the battlements of the tier;

lute song off the blames. Moaning mini-
symphonics underwrite maze blazing of cries
in the mids of my faces . . .

-dict no dirty crowd, taut; taughts,
held and slackened to twirl, waver-

songing

II

Cooling, she might hear you
sing and *know* the same words
and shift.
          Cash it now and every blip
is a dizzy how. Propelled
into a cringe, wrapped
in a growl:

the way you mock your blands

III

Mute up your factitious sensation

(even a ring of breath to kill

Transmute a crazed phrase of male hysterics

Break up this song into this gut-voiced holding

IV

Bounce a pebble voice on the
waves of this smile could then
if the sinking full-bowled
potential point of inform

Poison emotion. Floors crawl
a new song, doesn't fluff? A
strange stress on not-speech.
Hats on your horns gentlemen!

Ease a sample hammer
on the fall, blast over the stock.
Repeats; repeat tobacco-toned town;
the voice in my shivering circle.

V

Black Kansas, sit! Sudden guitar
gets it odderly

Hear those folded arms and clarity –
the doors of deception off-beats up-beat a
croak to the full;

risking flats affirm music

space him still low

spread to the lowest in time
to the admissible

last syllable cymbal out(→)s

28 MAY 1998

A Dirty Poem and A Clean Poem for Roy Fisher

for Roy Fisher 2
mayday98
Study 1
Twentieth Century Blues 59

1

The building was not 'backed by glowering indigo, browned
by the day and its frigid chaos', or whatever discourse
I'd once pasted it up on. Stripped out for allegory, its voiceover
prized each ethical chill. Sliding doors sluiced me
past welcome into publicity, security. Suspicion. Outside,
a police helicopter lowered in that replica New Labour Mayday
    sky
without cloud. We're up to see the Audi in the remoulded cheese
    grater
as clearly as the rusted Christmas trees down the embankment!

Be Here Now is etched into the handless clock face
on the deserted railway platform that promises late delivery
of what could be some special trick of a lusty kitsch.
Note headless female manikins at attention by the beds
in the department store window for the boniest of sex acts.
Fictive spans. What discourse could face this down, I ask,
facing up to what I might never simply call myself.
                     I never
could love something without a face on it.

2

Bolting the canal's chaos beneath the night's faceless want

Haunts another category

To re-tell the job you've paid oncoming readers

Flattened out

Under the bridge a stroke as historic as now

All moons dusk the day's falling

Waste as a spectral tick in a dusty box

Create strange beings that will image

What might become stretched out almost anywhere

MAY/NOVEMBER 1998

A Dark Study for Lee Harwood

for Lee Harwood 2
Study 2
Articulates 6
Twentieth Century Blues 60

Before work each morning, a walk round the lake. To observe: a
hole in thin ice; a lone birdwatcher

He looks up from the desk. Chatter. Nobody there, only
discarded drawings around the room; looks into another life:
the life squeezed out of these birds, as half-parrots, blob or
outline

No escape from 'God's feathered fairies

(you'd have found a poem hanging alongside the painting at the
Royal Academy in 1885

for several decades past, a taxonomy in flight: quarter-parrots,
or less, an abandoned sketch-line, or two

Love: a perfect claw round a hollow bone

Dreams of shrieking rainbow birds, yet silent as butterflies, a
soft breath of plumage. Of dark ornithomantic rites:

a ripped crop's message, the gizzard's bitter reply

In a house commanding a view of the Mersey, its last inhabitant
Emma the maiden scion of a proud family of Liverpool ship
owners, the painting entombed

In his study with his motionless focus upon Verisimilitude, the
Absolute Parrot, his exemplary effigies button-eyed, musty

trussed on the desk like Darwin's finches

Nameless servants blur in bucolic photographs of the grounds of Sudley House, semi-visible labour stacking hay

'In business as in contemplation, there is always an Elsewhere, an Otherwise

He cannot now find the words to settle the whole enterprise beyond the title: *'Recapitulation*

Facts are quiet. They resonate; only you can reply.

A slave girl stripped to the waist to reveal for the camera – somebody else's idea of memory – the evolutionary distinctiveness and stage of her race

(her name was Delia. She was born in the Americas, although her father, also photographed, originated in the Congo

appears to be crying, but has only perhaps moved her eyes in defiance of the command to sit still

'My first sighting of a Kakapo ground my theories to fine dust, sprinkled it across my pages. . . . six precious days lost travelling to that killing!

Everything she sees is bequeathed to you one way or another

A Treatise on Parrots by Henry Stacey Marks, oil on canvas (42 5/8 x 30 1/8 in.), bought by George Holt in 1886 for £525 (no bill extant

Parrot-coal chatters in the grate. An unseen hand silently rekin-
dles, keeps it alight for days, without warmth

Somewhere within the dark study the sound of what might be
sobbing

1999

For the Continuity Terminator

Mute Salutes 4
Melting Borders 5
Articulates 7
Empty Diary 1999
Twentieth Century Blues 61

My labia flip up between my hips like a Sumo's nuts

He's chiselled me into his identity parade, lost me in fragility's totter, guilty as style

Hardliners want to gun down Mr Universe; he used to lift our veils

(wherever my hundred sisters are now

he looks like a businessman about to be executed and we're to weep bitter self-enjoyings on his mandrake miracle

(he says

The Team commits Itself the Universe is Immortal

suffering to watch me watching the silk tie heaving on his rapidly panting chest; I can't guess the number of particles necessary to make one Butoh Butch!

Don't laugh! a punchline is exactly that. Slapstick

I don't recall my hand extending across the abyss to grasp the Flexibomber's yarrow stalk fingers

But now my presence queens him and, though a moniker will mean one thing, a Lewinsky will always mean something else!

Something else the ideogram means shakes the drips as she
inscribes the book famously smiling

She's anyone's mascara streak blinks the lips without parole

Jokes stick to her heaving pinstripe like diseases shot on pollen

a strangler's hands claw a risk of survival in the cooling of rela-
tions that followed the female infanticide moratorium

as well-adjusted as my brastraps and delicious blooms

*The 'Accused' is brain dead but accused of crimes committed before she
was born*

Then she stopped breathing naturally but made spermy mole-
cules drip from her eyes and ears at once

the ethics of signature scribbled out in the blows of dedication

I'm taken but not shaken

('It shudders me onto several planes of consciousness at once,'
he tells himself

shaking *this* baby until her brains rattle

Then she stopped breathing naturally and made liquid circular
trails with a fingertip wound around each sorrow

'I wish *I'd* written *Empty Diaries*, but I wouldn't have dared

(she hears herself saying

I'm a sexylipped handmaid, squeezing contaminated balls of spacetime to produce fresh spunk for the Muses

if I forget to file the verses of that esteemed male guest, then I'll be forced to kill myself by smoking my bones into brittle dust-jackets

The outlawed dildos of Alabama moan her woes, and echo back her sighs

MARCH 13 1999

31 Basalt Wind-chimes for the Window-Box of Earthly Pleasures

The End of the Twentieth Century 2
Implosive Samples 2
Human Dust 5
Twentieth Century Blues 64

O

Not a book of ayres not a solid monotone. An eye. An ear. Willed to pleasure, let's take a note for a walk across the humming strings. Human

O

Human dust on which history overdosed twice (at least) in one century

O

This dance means bumping into things, yet jump back from the path of Creation's clockwork

O

Atheism does not exist because god invented it! A force to vent: *Velopoesis*

O

A single voice on a single page – there's music enough. The newspaper vendor cries: '*Echo . . . Echo*

O

Plonk (see **plunk**); his rush of pleasure haunts the paths of sense with sensation

[105]

O

But that spooky charm is not earthly goodness as one would want to know it!

O

The fat, melting, dissipates more energy than it conserves. As does repeating the spiky line that unravels into a force larger than its parts

O

There ain't no way they can replace this vacuum I created in human history

O

The discipline of hazard and high quality shoots aloft the victims' pitiable admiration that builds *under* the crust of pain while Creation adjusts its ancient braces

O

The Author of Bangs, against which we nuzzle the footnote of something like human justice. If he is condemned to time, push the eye out and climb out. as from a shell into the bright dream of tomorrow. Obtain your liberty and fiery scope, a phoenix of 'Socio-Pleasurableness'!

O

Routes bloomed across bound wastes: up to off and over and out until they feel like jelly: *'Your faire lookes enflame*

O

A sensation that is almost an emotion an aubade an algorithmic simulation

O

(a vacuum

O

Suck parody? Constituents of pleasure are not to be taken for granted

O

(sings:) *Dear, if you change, I'll melt away like lard!*

O

Jaunty now, where the lyrics are dainty. Its opposite, in semantic counterpoint, a miraculous parliament!

O

Keep Creation dramatic and didactic, that's the trick! Each single eye is plugged tight with transformations

O

The strange persistence of the meanings of certain words through centuries. Which syllable shall we elongate to quench again with love?

O

The **right** to pleasure, as under statute. A **unit** of pleasure, its animus (Who needs devils with gods like that?

O

Born again, to free Poetic Fury? Dust caught in bees' wax. Turn your lamp up in unbelief. Pleasure has no balance

O

to catch the almost-involuntary spurt of semen or the spiritualist who contacted Bradlaugh after death to catch his confession! Weightless epiphanies

O

'Shine him off that window!' This goes *with* saying

O

Who said purity wove their words, advertising just one admired synthesis?

O

Has an oath truer currency for being underwritten by fear and by stone-eyed defenders of monuments? Cease to be pleasuring response is lost until it sings far from a said

O

Shifting rime   that easie flatterer   a cat chasing a fly

O

Pleasure's twin. Standing by his word, a god of flesh she forms

O

Clocking form, the infectious eye catches pleasure being caused. The unhasty song when responsibility descants as response

O

The sigh of a cosmos, cooling, expanding; the resurrection of an idea of the word *as*

O

Unseal the lid at last! A chamber of twentieth century echoes rings. Soiled prose-songs of Velopolis

JUNE 1999

From the English

Electronic letters winked the news from the Stakeholder Tower; swans flew by like messengers from another world

A field factory of kerchiefed women threshed and piled the urinous corn against their rhyming hems

He slipped past the uranium-graphite rods. into the Netherworld, rivet eyes in the glow

The incisiveness of our colour-coded marginalia, lists of Craft Guilds, a cactus world of barbed tongues, citizens layered and flayed like old election posters on the blistered walls of post-industrial squares

Each twitch of the Leader is choreographed, leaps of laughter, flares of rage

Biplanes wheel over the basilicas and wine lodges to the sound of a once fashionable tango

Red moves in the river as red should, diluted. Uncut tongues smelted in George's lyrical furnace declare that the heavy, wing-less evening glides to a split pomegranate sunset

Pearl spills her bra, sprawled on her stomach across the bed, clacking her heels like castanets behind her ears. The maimed body of English culture is too tragic a theme for her bed! The wisdom of nobody in particular sings:

'The nightingales of Reform are resting in the Cuckoos' Nests
(*this eulogy is composed in accordance with specifications ratified at
the* 19th *Great Consultation of Amnesia*

Pearl the Slut lives in the smoked-sausage stench of a one room
flat. The sun beats competitively down on the frost outside. Her
Economic Plan is one foot in a stiletto, the other in a dirty boot,
dust shaken contemptuously at her gaping supervisor in the
pigswill canteen

The Prosecutor has been given Pearl's proverbial rabbit but still
wants her unspeakable hen, as she shifts her hams (*watch your
language, translation is the third oldest profession*) in tight
Transatlantic jeans during a three-quarters sex scene. Singers
melt mid-verse

Rubbery mouths turn inside out to vomit bilious panegyrics
onto our petalled river. 'We are a fairytale

retold in thick contradictory voices howling over the capital at
its Festival of Rebirth, while women like Lorraine swell magic
fruit on the boughs with incantations before they pluck them

Pearl married a Party Gnome to escape the unblinking eye that
some rachitic small-town Cyclops had trained on her. She had
been meat jelly once for George, round the back of the Snow
Flake Café

They trod a hymn to their undying love in the drift, an acrostic
of the Leader's name. Robyn's well-fed cackle proved she could
only ever, at best, turn out a slum landlady, teeth reflected in
the bonnet of her Bentley

Girls fainting with hunger still poked breadsticks through the
wires for the POWs

We learnt to count by computing the bullet holes in her leg. The Fleet was paid in riverbanks, as my old Dad used to say (whatever he meant by it). The tourist centre gleams

Bulls topple from the heroes' plinth in the Meat Industry Zone at the feet of the Maidens of Economic Advancement

It can only be built on bottom-up inspiration that looks down, she said, with the lowered head of a thousand qualified *buts*!

Today's union bosses are well read, put to bed in vests, with bowls for their spewings. Pearl

Pearl, the pillow smells of Pearl

Pearl is last spotted, knee deep in snow, looking at the new road signs that the security services have garlanded, as though she were the saint

This is a Stone Throwing Revolution, and George says he will cast first! The full-bloodied, deep-juiced moon gloats, aflame like a hayrick in the English Civil War

The great cause now is to serve something mundane and self-serving, the Metaphysics of the Bone Age

The Stakeholder Orchestra demilitarises, bribing the Guild for a Reeling Life and an Easy Death with four bottles of White Lightning. Inside the stuffing of the party's Teddy Bear mascot: the ferrule fist. Let there be more than one light. A flower-girl (black and white) presented on the steps of Chequers

the same, among the myriad spheres of dandelion heads, the breeze unpicking spore. Whose boot will kick through them, in judgement, terrible and tetchy? Robyn's bile leaks over our identity papers. Purge trial

Summer parks where convicted homosexuals meet the drunks, contaminating fruit-head guests before empty plates, spitting pips, juice (that roughly translates as: *they contort in an unrepeatable dance that means no more than the footprints they leave in the flowerbeds*

Jayne lands a part in the folk-rock opera *Lefty*. 'Nice world,' quips Roger, 'if you can get it

'You fucker!' she says, for the first time in English art the speech of the riff raff and scum who hang around our suburban trains

The table cluttered with the opulence of a tax free Weekend Cottage

Roger wants to plug her mouth with flesh. This First Minotaur (*Minister?*) presses her down onto the sofa, as she awaits his sudden thrust from behind, his blood stream an arrow shower, obeying history rather than the history books

Her hands blossom in bunches of moon flowers in the party political sky. Shrapnel marks on stone announce the visitation of Progress at some point in her still mobile history

Effigies laugh like gutters throughout England, mocking our shoes which squeak with embarrassment, brushed to a blush

The Interrogation scene is panned by the critics with its chorus of *ditto ditto ditto* as Roger denies each trumped up charge. He finishes mid-sentence because the tune runs out of notes

AUGUST 1999

The Sacred Tanks of Dagenham

The Materialization of Soap 1947, 4
Impositions 3
Articulates 10
Twentieth Century Blues 66

for Keith Tuma and Nate Dorward

once Pearl pricks the two chops in the sizzling pan restaurant
music she says

crouched towards the postcards outside the tobacconist's
George lives and loves it all though iceless

not the corner *ABC* spelt out of emptiness nor the mobile
library of American magazines

an abstract noun fogs the capital city until the breeze's caprice

looks could kill and still be made to look good

packets of *Creamola* in windows searched after their sewing class
digests with gusto

absence and abstinence

leading to orderly queues or queues of asylum orderlies wheel-
ing their own reflections into the chilly English Channel

the frozen symbol of nationhood empire's dissolution home
made

eat what you see hell of damaged stock half-price turnips will
find their way to Heaven

through multiple hardbaked soil

creak for milk over the bathtub she poured coffee in case who will buy air

(selling air

a high wind bites through the worn threads of jogging army girls a state bard recites through his beard and his beads of sweating half rhymes

Pearl's first wrinkle faces the wringer

buxom corn maidens with gleaming washtubs await the dispensary of grubby propensities to consume the word 'democracy' doesn't creak through our rafters

too high for worship

her finger tickles his meat balls his organ is an old widow's well-paid wellwisher

George's wick sticks up in sticky appreciation

bangs like a barn door for the girls' buoyancy against the oppressive clouds there's a cut out shape where Pearl was washing George's smalls

threatening blank pages at the backs of ration books ready for whatever is fewer

winners catch the cooling mint flavoured newsprint scrolls from Dagenham to Dagestan

labels *Individual Balconies* small squares on the brushed magnificence the *Sacred Tanks* open thin ribs of land dress for talk everything is mean and means little

unrelated to a shortage the Sydenham band has disbanded the
saxophones swing in the heat near the public well

(skilfully carrying water jugs for miles on their heads

the woman in foxfurs explains the marvels of the snow on the
field of blood meaning itself subject to this economy

the clacking abacus drum stores the few apples' stories as docu-
ments and dockets

cleansing invisibility hides in Hyde Park from the laughter is
deaf but vital hands perhaps even George's weeping penis wash-
ing Pearl

will emigrate to Canada to begin again

doing her business lust flashes like George's shape has been
pruned from his allotment of pure time regeneration trumpets
over the city in each tree kippers and cider roused them to it

outside Timothy Whites they clatter the hardware like Gene
Krupa tubs in his straps a post-war blur of rematerialising Hero
nervously waits to deNazify the English East Midlands of its
thin-lipped officials

abed in the crystal crematoria of recent history

the past's persistence we knitted our way to victory and now
we're eating shit 50 million flies can't be wrong

('and now Pearl will croak a few bars for barter

George sniffs his way through her fat negotiating hothouse
grapes gleaming bladders in greengrocer's immortal calligra-
phy spelling flowers for his staff car

plenty is the finger that touches Pearl's meat for once they'll
recognise this attempt

to cojoin George's triumphal offal language falling from sign-
posts (*we work or want*; no

says George: *we*

want

work

to provide a validating ethos for Man kicking in the night ('here
he goes again

a bombsite ripe for conjuring him once more in plentiful
Kodachrome against her shins

whose thighs make a necklace of pearl clouds in a grey sky
building plots national assistance

near the dosshouse round the back of the Palace of the Winds

17 AUGUST 1999

Say

Say 1
Articulates 11
Twentieth Century Blues 68

Say I people these squares of glass

playmate of the impossible, I listen to your howl

across the floating gardens between the equipment units and
the living units

Your metabolic rhythms are coerced by the nebulous obsession
that discourses through ill-adjusted air conditioning, counter

points the smashings of workmen disgorging the shell where
the Old Widow Marx once dwelt. Singular planes

of tilted glass reflect dead sky. Say hello. I want you to see this

as a book again, or as a parliament or ministry of justice build-
ing that looks like a nuclear power plant (There is a voice

it says '*beauty*

though the streetjive of postmodernism is policed by the
dictionary of modernity. It might recruit you

to causes that remain inimical to your judgement

or government; this is everyday life slipping along the radius of
the everyday world. Go away. Say

This is no Palace of Art, not even a map of it. Don't say: the solution
is dynamite

the blocks collapsing squarely into a frozen cloud of their own
dust. Say:

demonstrate your intelligence, stamping the pages with the
ictus of identity and contra-

diction, the space now only inhabited by the hidden inter-
change of knowledge and its otherwise

Say: you scratch the veneer of an authoritarian static fit and
what do you find, when the next drunk, or the girl

next door, positioned on the radial, smiles sourly or sweetly, and
asks you to justify your discursive habits

(and the income it provides from its patented buzzword

what are you going to say? *Once there were formal*

houses on the main road, informal ones nearer the lake, and a few prac-
tices that you're allowed in between, a handful of dialect words and a
fistful of proscribed gestures? Say: this is meant

to be a model for communicative action as motivation

as alignment

as celebration as actualisation

for those who snap the snare

for those who refuse to exploit experience as the supplement of
history

as a bloodbath after one of the hostages says The Wrong Word

The path is formed by the various buildings that stretch either
side of the path that was not there until the grammar just about

made it to the full stop. Say

you say something and *I'll* reply: *Dialogue*

and the Everyday

SEPTEMBER–OCTOBER 1999

In an Unknown Tongue

BOOK ONE

George loosens his blood-red tie and they begin. The lower beings have contested the Upper Beings and they hope to take the trophy back beneath the lines that hold the nether world intact.

'I leapt up the steps from the Seine to Rouen Cathedral but he was no longer by my side. Some street preacher had grabbed him by the shoulder and was promising to cast out his demons. It was about this time that I knew he would go over to the "other side".'

Collapses on a bench under the right-angled legend: 'Ashbury'/'Haight'. Several historical details seem inaccurate and the edges of the crowd are beginning to fray. The Volkswagon guns its engine: *Peace* bubble-lettered on the shivering bonnet.

(He was getting pedantic; 'Wimples *like* oakleaves mean: wimples *and* oakleaves.')

'On deck, I smoked and relaxed. He whistled a spy-movie. The ship was slipping behind the scratched curtain.'

The line down her face gives her a third eye through which she can see the frozen watch hanging over the gunwales like the stalactites she conjures there. Instead of a name this vessel carries a health warning that calibrates her as its lethal dose.

Oracular signs on the mountain pass barnacled into icy immobility.

The boys try to tempt her but *she* will be doing the tempting, thank you very much! The jiffy-bags Pearl perches on contain vacutainers of frozen sperm, tributes to her crimson lips, her pointed breasts under the crimson gown that conceals, yet reveals, enough for the boys' muffled ejaculations: flatfooted hand-jobs for imaginary leg-liftings, gown-droppings, a backbone of tingles, a snowdust of orgasm.

Crusoe meets his portent over the nets. Looking the wrong way for an instant ounces of evolutionary software are wiped from his hard drive.

Gripping onto the rigging over the bucking sea, its own animate nightmare, that's the poor bastard they named Lucky! A cigarette between the fingers of each trigger-happy hand. Another moment's lapse and he'll slip into irony.

Her red lips, too, her blood-red shawl, adjust the filters of power. Cut glass nymphs with vulture wings call out to assassins on the bridge to drop anchor in the pools of her tragic eyes. Her freckled arms, her white-gloved hands, will try to hold the world together as it spatters apart on the cream upholstery.

Glints off a silver fuselage on the dusty air-strip. Pearl and Lorraine grin over their clutches of hand luggage and foxfurs. Ropes slither at their feet. Groaning men grip their empty bellies and retch. George, or what should be George, carries a loaf with his luggage, and he could break it to distribute among the hunched grey figures. It is election year.

She opens her blouse, but nobody looks, except the Ancients posed above her next to the broken masthead. Dead men have drudged here, she thinks; the living are obsessed with their red wine and smoke-rings. She might as well sing 'Twentieth Century Blues'. Later, in his lordship's bathroom her famous fanny will open like a lobster's claw, she thinks, to piss an ocean into his even more famous mouth.

BOOK TWO

A crossbow shoots a Schlitz bottle clean from Elzadie's head.
Those lips that made Amorica shatter.

He gave up the throne for this dancing deaths-head, plays dice
on deck, for the double orchestra will never be asked to play on
this Ark. Lank sails hang over rotten beams, as lifeless as his
trousers over the back of the chair (he calls his throne) for the
parlour game he names Coronation Night.

Jiving for pearls with his slicked-back blue Superman hair –
suddenly The Hero grips his neck and falls to the rock and roll
deck where those who have long bopped have dropped. Spurt
your Bud!

China cat smile! Chinese silk dreams of the Birdman's starlit
axe-blow night. From the nest to the egg-cup. The orange tree
potted in dog shit prose.

Penelope awaits Odysseus by the Hollywood poolside, with the
embarrassing six year old and the dog. Through the polar
columns of the Temple to the Medusa, she has a clear view of
. the Ithacan sea, and beyond: the sperm-fucked waves, the
whores' hair spore of the cresting, nipple-bobbing, cunt-snap-
ping ocean. No Man idles by the watch, not daring to take the
heroic plunge.

'Thirties modernism in Beirut seemed somehow right: tall
enough to be a look-out, yet close enough to decipher the blue
chalk on the whitewashed walls below: the command to vanish.
A battalion of my father's Arab henchmen dead drunk on the
floor was a near perfect cover.'

Waves net across the skein. Cloudy sails in slants of sleet. Pale sun interferes with the sky's blank message. The wrong grave.

The dangling corpse of Jack's jilted queen toes the biting ocean. Jackie had written to her mother every week about his cruelty, his strange occult habits, his masculine verse. She was the girl next year.

Perfect cover, as a dwarf reporter for the *Morning Post!*

He wears a crow-black tie so often that he ends up being called out to funerals at all hours. Pulling rope, the mariners' feet tangle among the limbs of those who have died at this task: staring still. It is his job to close these eyes during the breaks between shifts.

'He called me out to play his spy-game on the veranda. With his little eye he'd sent dozens to their deaths for something beginning with C. In the forest a woodcutter's chainsaw sang like a muezzin, long notes and halftones. History was closing in.'

Eyes, their last glimmers fading, bodies fallen in configurations of least resistance like a Duke's underwear.

On the shore, Isolde walks the dog between the treacherous black rocks. She pulls the white fur round her, a polar bear against the gangrenous dawn. Tristan hangs on for dear life, in the crow's nest, to the rope that holds his reality together. The sea boils and hisses, either side of the crashing prow.

BOOK THREE

Two women rest their wings, and their tongues, which are also wings.

Drifted sober into this line of defence: 'beached' boats in mud. A stain that could be a man on horseback, a cardiac flare in the chest, or a facecloth of guilt.

Mistake any gnarled tree trunk for a leg. The Angels of Reason chorus over the Yachting Marina, where the research is financed by laundered drug money. To breakfast is to chew nails out of rotten timber.

A host of chorusing pill bottles tumbles across the doctor's desk. Decked. 'Death has not been a door to us, but a rubbish-chute,' she sings. Shells of human beings, their organs in neat pots behind her.

Fungal clouds infect the azure. Beowulf's bier, upon towering seas. Barged back by the bullying waves. The angle of light upon the skeleton conjures expressive eyes into its empty sockets. Deliverance is judgement, a thick blanket of lines to shroud us.

He sank beneath the lines. Spirited in a rowing boat from the shipwreck of the singular, he will be reborn, spouting gallons of seawater, on the shores of Utopia.

Or: Puking his passage across the Channel like a bilge-pump, the Creature would travel, under false papers, to Vienna, where he would vanish, a veritable Adam before Eve. But first he must brave language, the ejaculating waves.

Beatrice arrives bewitched, bewildered, a baby in her propeller arms; her son carries *The Beano*. The theology she utters to reporters is so astonishing that even the airport porters rubber-neck.

Soldiers throw a boy over the bridge parapet and machinegun the water. The UN swerves the post-colonial highways in gleaming Toyotas, the effluent of an advertisement they claim not to be in. Deep in the forest, the Dark Figure calls the last militia-man to experience his final blade.

The last woodchopper won't burst into Granny's Greenhouse tonight; the wolves' eyes flicker at the glass. He is stopped by a man he barely recognises. They shake hands, talk treachery round to loyalty with a few semantic reversals. Codenames reveal only gender. The little girl is a pile of bones but the cat still purrs in the secret photographic darkroom.

'This place is bugged by my former wives,' George whispers outside his new dacha, tending the shrine he has built to Pearl.

Tied to the mast like Odysseus or Turner, his eyes are filled with nothing but these strange women with huge prosthetic ears that are also sex organs. These women, even Isolde, masturbate by rubbing the ears together over the tops of their heads. Even crucified like him – he's the third or fourth Adam – they could generate their own pleasure still.

Her polar fur wrapped about her, broken boots for her broken body, she treads seed pods into the soft tarmac, as she leaves the walled Seaport (if you misread the brewery's castellation). A wisp of irony feathers the empurpled underbelly of the evening sky, but she will miss it, as ever.

12 OCTOBER 1999

Catacaustic

for Tom Raworth

Some Words 2
Study 3
Articulates 15
Twentieth Century Blues 73

Numbers polished petrol back to his room

changed

continuously in the swell clouds flickered the afternoon stalactites up a stone cracked open leaving

searching

the docks map a blank plan destroyed 50s flights of steps to work at two chairs

scribbled falls flickered to speak near rushing table

remembered the last news labelled a quick sketch in the ejected

hold sides of wire tiles

between air spits on the windows happy with

lines appeared to hold breathing

from the real shutters switched the day's dog shit off as the cleaners run down the central hoardings pick up

endless photographs of xerox stone hits roofs to shout down bright red shoes the shutters scrap

of blue steps through his head at the bottom of decay dark grey and calm eyes and mouth and flash

of the starts of ends and adding in paper twists loud

real

fingers approach being the last poem

stated his method.

19 December 1999

The Push Up Combat Bikini

Coda 4

IM 11

Empty Diary 2000

Twentieth Century Blues 75

Such turned out to be the eternity the poet promised me, the bastard
ANGELA CARTER

All the king's men shot their horses. Stuck in your silence,
fumbling your authority around shutters to lock passion in
with your mumbling sound track – it echoes you – a bundle

of themes thrown like runes. I trust myself, shaped a viola in
renal error, and pierced; teeth in that slit as near-miss melodies
snap at your fingers. Each verb

flaps loose on your *oeuvre* shut down like an illegal dive, you're
coming over all female. The conceit's too clean 'Out of the push
up, they're a let down, deposits that

won't quite register, though banked on your looking, sniffing
eroticism off dirty shifts, smudges of pelts; I slip an ought, drop
a stitch *Hot gushes signal his retreat, never alone*

with pokes of spermatic blessing misguided by all that comes to mind
That's enough of your impoverished single prayer *(mechanical
benedictions from my Virgin Mary Dildo* 'Was that a rich girl?

Every time I open my mouth out comes a manifesto of a new
literary movement! Was that a poem, curling round you or its
echo, nerves ajangle on syntax's opening,

taking me, and taking me for somebody else, performed out, as
you've pushed me up between the lines? What might a poem be,
elsed? Sewn up by your equation so you

can dunk your aching, lived-in balls in ink and roll them across the page (hide the man! I'm your Voice-Drudge, shagged out Muse, please take me over you this last time

your eyes sucking at the nipples you fixed up. Whistle me Pearl, whisper me off, now I'm a big register on your retina, breathlessly weaving love into a puppet prick

that can be choreographed. Petrified flesh pivots on golden heels. The umbilicus slips out on schedule; I'm pegged on that line to George's fructifying semiotic stuff (*and nonsense* 'If the next

woman to part risks Absolute Emotion, I'm little more than an instance of a fuck fucking (**he said** (she said (*who says* a ventriloquist's huffing tongues my clitoris, *it speaks!*

with a style that stales, its trim priesthood of taking hard parts. Skin flickers within each saying weighted with testicular pomp, hot spurts deferred under your synchronised chorus of sweating wankers

dedicated to the memory of Barry MacSweeney, with a different Pearl

2000

Notes

Tin Pan Arcadia forms a sizeable portion of *Twentieth Century Blues*, a 75 part
series of poems written between 1989 and 2000 (the first and last poems
may be read here). With small exceptions, the rest of the project may
be found in the following books: *The Flashlight Sonata*, Stride, Exeter,
1993, *Empty Diaries*, Stride, Exeter, 1998, *The Lores*, Reality Street, 2003,
which are parts 6, 24 and 30 respectively. The following pamphlets are
also parts of the project: *Neutral Drums* (with Patricia Farrell), Writers
Forum, 1999, *The End of the Twentieth Century*, Ship of Fools, 2002, and
Ocean Green: Homage to Jack B Yeats, forthcoming, which are parts 37, 63,
and 40 respectively. The poetics of the project are discussed in parts 14
and 18, which appear in my *Far Language : Poetics and Linguistically
Innovative Poetry 1978–1997*, Stride Research Documents, 1999. Its index,
part 74, is available as *Links in Ink* from Ship of Fools. The project is
described as a 'net/(k)not – work(s)' in that the poems are not just
numbered sequentially but involve multiple titles which enable
'strands' to overlap and extend, as may be demonstrated by the various
'Empty Diaires' and 'Killing Boxes' in this volume.

Fucking Time: Selected Notes and Resources (1994)

Title – Aubrey's *Brief Lives* (Life of Franciscus Linus), quoted in Adlard, p.78:
'The Smashing of the Phallic Dials': '. . . broken all to pieces . . . by the
Earl of Rochester, Lord Buckhurst, Fleetwood Sheppard, etc. coming in
from their revels. "What!" said the Earl of Rochester, "doest thou stand
here to —— Time?" Dash they set to work.'

Song 1 – 'Love and Life, a Song', Wilmot, p. 65
'Song' ('By all Loves soft, yet mighty Pow'rs'), ibid, p. 67
'Appetite'/'Aversion': Hobbes, Book 1, Ch. VI.

Song 2 – 'The Mock Song', Wilmot, p. 69
'Satyr', ibid., p. 6

Song 3 – 'Satyr', Wilmot, p. 6
Letter to Rochester from Savile, Treglown, p. 62
Mrs Frances Stewart became Britannia on coins of the realm, but the
point is more general.
'Incorporeal body': Hobbes, Book1

Song 4 – The suggestive impression in the grass I owe to Charles II's poem to
Frances Stewart: 'I pass all my time in a shady old grove'.
References to 'leading the coranto' and 'Mercury's frauds' are lost; prob-
ably Rochester's letters, or Hobbes?
'Dowry snatches': At one level, Rochester's abduction of Elizabeth
Malet; Adlard, p. 33. Both Aubrey and Pepys record the affront.
'Shutters, mid-stage.//She spreads her fan.' See Etherege, particularly

Act Three, Scene 1. The character Dorimont was modelled either upon Rochester or upon a model of Rochester.

Song 5 – 'External things', 'running over an alphabet/to start a rhyme', Hobbes, Book 1.
'Tarse' (penis) 'arse', as in 'In the Fields of Lincoln Inns' (possibly by Sedley), Wilmot, p. 53

Song 6 – Letter from Rochester to Savile, Treglown, p. 66
'Bougre': Letter from Rochester to Savile, ibid, p. 158
The bugger who suggested the description was Titus Oates; see also letter from Rochester to Savile, ibid, p. 232

Resources

Adlard, J (ed.) 1974, *The Debt to Pleasure*, John Wilmot, the Earl of Rochester, Carcanet: Manchester.
Etherege, G, *The Man of Mode*, in Gosse (ed.) 1964, *Restoration Plays*, Dent: Herts.
Hobbes, T. 1651 (1962) *Leviathan*, Fontana: Glasgow.
Treglown, J. (ed.) 1980, *The Letters of John Wilmot, Earl of Rochester*, Basil Blackwell: Oxford.
Wilmot, J. Earl of Rochester, 1680? *Poems on Several Occasions*, Antwerpen (sic)

Cover art work, by Patricia Farrell, incorporates a design from her images for the first edition of *Fucking Time* (Ship of Fools, 1994).

Printed in the United Kingdom
by Lightning Source UK Ltd.
101288UKS00001B/406-408